Taking Notes

A Quick Guide

COMPLETE
TEST PREPARATION INC.
WWW.TEST-PREPARATION.CA

ISBN-13: 9781772452730

Version 8 April 2025

ABOUT COMPLETE TEST PREPARATION INC.

Why Us?

The Complete Test Preparation Team has been publishing high quality study materials since 2005, with a catalogue of over 145 titles, in English, French, Spanish and Chinese, as well as ESL curriculum for all levels.

To keep up with the industry changes, we update everything all the time!

And the best part?

With every purchase, you're helping people all over the world improve themselves and their education. So thank you in advance for supporting this mission with us! Together,
we are truly making a difference in the lives of those often forgotten by the system.

Charities that we support

https://www.test-preparation.ca/charities-and-non-profits/
You have definitely come to the right place.
If you want to spend your valuable study time where it will help you the most - we've got you covered today and tomorrow.

CONTENTS

7 **Reading**

Reading for Different Purposes   8

Speed Up or Slow Down?   11

Finding the Main Idea   12

Main Idea Exercises   13

18 **Taking Notes**

Tips for Taking Notes   19

Outline Method   26

Split-Page Method   31

Charting Method   33

Mapping Method   34

5 Methods for Taking Notes   35

36 **Taking Notes Practice**

Cornell Method - Passage 1   39

Split Page Method - Passage 1   40

Mapping Method - Passage 1   41

Charting Method - Passage 1   42

Cornell Method - Passage 2   45

Split Page Method - Passage 2   46

Charting Method - Passage 2   47

Mapping Method - Passage 2   48

Outlining Method - Passage 3   50

Cornell Method - Passage 3   52

Split Page Method - Passage 3   53

Charting Method - Passage 3   54
Mapping Method - Passage 3   55
Tips for Taking Notes   60

61   **Common Abbreviations & Symbols**
How to Study from your Notes   64
How to Study from Textbooks   69

70   **Studying Textbooks**

74   **Conclusion**

76   **Online Resources**

https://www.test-preparation.ca

Published by
Complete Test Preparation Inc.
Victoria BC Canada

Visit us on the web at
https://www.test-preparation.ca

Feedback

We welcome your feedback. Email us at feedback@test-preparation.ca with your comments and suggestions. We carefully review all suggestions and often incorporate reader suggestions into upcoming versions. As a Print on Demand Publisher, we update our products frequently.

 Find us on Facebook

www.facebook.com/CompleteTestPreparation

PART I
READING

READING RATES FOR DIFFERENT PURPOSES

Reading for different purposes means adjusting your reading rate

Different Purposes for Reading

(Why are you reading?)

- To get the general idea?
- To learn, point by point, in detail?
- To find one point or fact in something you've already read?
- To entertain yourself?

WHY ARE YOU READING?

What type of material are you reading?

- How difficulty of the material for you?
- Is it easy?
- Is it difficult?
- How familiar are you with the subject?
- Do you have some background on the subject?
- Is it totally new?

CHANGING YOUR READING SPEED

Reading efficiently means changing your reading speed as often as required.

For example, if you are reading a science book about Mars. At the beginning, there is a short story about exploring Mars. You can read this quickly. After the story, there is information about the chemistry of the martian surface. Slow down and read carefully. Or, you may not be interested in the chemistry at all, so you can skim this part quickly.

If you are reading this book to find out about NASA exploration of mars, you can skim the first two sections until you get to the section on NASA exploration.

Depending on why you are reading your speed will change.

WHY?	SPEED
Reading for main idea only	FAST
Reading for fun	FAST
Reading to learn new material	SLOW
Find a fact or idea	FAST
Reading as 'art' e.g. poetry	SLOW

WHAT ARE YOU READING?

What kind of material are you reading? Depending on the type of material, you speed will change.

WHAT	SPEED
Difficult Vocabulary and ideas	SLOW
Subjects you already know	FAST
Technical reading	SLOW
Instructions or Directions	SLOW
Reading as 'art' e.g. poetry	SLOW

SPEED UP OR SLOW DOWN?

Certain words are clues, for you to either speed up or slow down your reading speed.

SPEED UP SIGNALS

- Any passage with no vocabulary blocks, no complicated sentences or ideas.

- A passage where you only want the most important idea.

- A passage that repeats or elaborates on something you already know.

- A passage that is not related to your purpose in reading.

SLOW DOWN SIGNALS

- New or difficult vocabulary or ideas.

- Details you want to remember.

- Subjects that are new to you.

- Directions that you need to follow exactly.

- Reading that refers to a picture or diagram where you have to shift between the reading and the diagram.

FINDING THE MAIN IDEA

Tips for finding the main idea

Once you find the topic, ask what the author is saying about the topic. Generally this is the main idea.

Most main ideas are at the beginning. Pay attention to the first one third of the passage. Often, but not always, the main idea is the first or second sentence.

Are there any ideas that are repeated, or re-stated? Generally this is the main idea.

Try it out!   Once you have found the main idea, ask yourself if the examples, reasons, statistics, studies, and facts in the passage support, explain or give evidence of your main idea.   If not – try again!

MAIN IDEA EXERCISES

PASSAGE 1

Instructions: Read the passage below, find the main idea, and write in the space provided.

During World War I, a number of severe shortages alerted the world's scientists to the need for synthetic or man-made materials. Thus by 1934, a research team headed by Wallace H. Carothers had developed the first synthetic fiber, called nylon. As it turned out, the development of nylon had a surprisingly profound effect on world affairs. True, its first use was in fashion, and in 1939, Dupont began marketing sheer nylon hose for women. Nylons were a spectacular hit and sold off the shelves almost immediately. But they disappeared with the coming of World War II, as nylon became essential to the war effort. It was used in everything from parachutes and ropes, to insulation and coat linings. Sadly Carothers never witnessed the impact of his creation. He committed suicide two years before the first pair of nylons ever went on sale.

What is the topic?

_____

_____

_____

What is the main idea?

_____

_____

_____

IMPORTANT FACTS IN THIS PASSAGE

Inventor of nylon - Wallace Carothers

Invented - 1934

1939 - sheer nylon hose – nylons

Used in WWII – parachutes, ropes, insulation, coat linings

Carothers committed suicide

PASSAGE #2

While she lived, the Mexican painter Frida Kahlo was known mainly as the wife of the famed muralist Diego Rivera. Yet in the decades since her death, Kahlo has become hugely famous in her own right and is probably now better known than her husband. In 1990, Kahlo became the first Mexican artist to break the one million mark at an auction. The vivid, self-portraits that Kahlo created in the thirties and forties continue to be widely sought after by collectors willing to pay high prices for her paintings. Although Kahlo is often described as a painter intent on exploring her own personal reality, many of her paintings include references to Mexico's political and social history. It's not surprising, then, that in 1985, the Mexican government publicly proclaimed her work a national treasure.

What is the topic?

_____

_____

_____

What is the main idea?

_____

_____

_____

Important facts in this passage

_____

_____

_____

_____

_____

PASSAGE #3

Every second, 1 hectare of the world's rain forest is destroyed. That's equivalent to two football fields. An area the size of New York City is lost every day. In a year, that adds up to 31 million hectares -- more than the land area of Poland. This alarming rate of destruction has consequences for the environment. Scientists estimate, for example, that 137 species of plant, insect or animal become extinct every day due to logging. In British Columbia, where, since 1990, thirteen rain forest valleys have been clearcut, 142 species of salmon have already become extinct, and the habitats of grizzly bears, wolves and many other creatures are threaened.

What is the topic?

_____

_____

_____

What is the main idea?

_____

_____

_____

Important facts in this passage

_____

_____

_____

_____

_____

Main Idea/Topic Exercise - Answers

Passage #2

Topic: Frida Kahlo
Main Idea: Frida Kahlo is more famous (well known) after her death than when she was alive.

Passage #3

Topic: Destruction of the rain forest
Main Idea: Fast destruction of the rain forest has

consequences for the environment.

PART 2
TAKING NOTES

TIPS FOR TAKING NOTES

Put Note-Taking at the top of your study skills list. A key elements in passing any course is taking good notes. To learn the required information, your notes need to be thorough and organized in a way that makes them easy to review later. For many students, however, note taking is a difficult task, and often notes have too little or too much information, or the wrong information to make them useful.

STRATEGIES AND TIPS TO DEVELOP GOOD NOTE TAKING HABITS:

Prepare The first tip for taking better notes is to prepare for the lecture. Read over the assigned material before class. This will give you some familiarity with the material to be covered and allow you to formulate any questions about that material in advance. This will help you take notes faster since it isn't the first time that you have heard about it.

Show up It's impossible to take great class notes if you don't go to class. Make sure you attend the first class because that's when the teacher will let you in on the course outline, and their expectations in terms of homework, class assignments and testing. You'll also get a good indication on how the course will be marked.

Keep showing up The best way to gather great notes for a class is to go to class every day. Aim for perfect attendance. Spending time with your teacher allows you to get to know his or her teaching style and allows you to understand what to study, and what the teacher is looking for in test answers. You may not actually make it to the end of the semester with perfect attendance, but if you shoot for perfect, then you have some room for the unexpected. This way you may have an attendance record of 98%, when you aimed for perfect. Nothing wrong with that!

Listen Taking good notes requires you to listen in class. Listening carefully enables you to pick up on points that may not be covered in the written material for the class. There will definitely be a lot of material that is only covered in the lectures. It also enables you to take better notes because you are able to hear the instructor say key words that help organize your notes. For example:

The instructor may emphasize certain points with tone, volume or gestures.

The instructor may use signal phrases like, "There are three reasons..." or, "There are two points of view..." These phrases alert you to significant points and help you structure your notes.

The instructor may review at the start of class or summarize at the end, giving you a chance to make sure you have the most important points.

Often professors will actually tell you what is going to be on the final exam!

If you do miss a class ... It's tough to miss a class, because the teacher is going to continue to the next thing and you may have missed a crucial part. Any material mentioned in class is eligible to appear in a future test. However, if you miss class, borrow notes from another student (one who takes good class notes).

This is an excellent reason to exchange contact information with at least two other students in each class. You never know when you'll need help catching up, and you don't want to wait until you are in a tight spot.

Your notebook
Don't underestimate the organizational power of your notebook. It's the central location to arrange your class information in a way that is easiest for you to understand. Learn to take great study notes in your notebook and take care not to lose it!

Choosing a notebook
The best type of notebook is a 3-ring binder type with loose-leaf paper.

A loose-leaf binder notebook also allows you to remove old notes from the notebook to make it less cumbersome to carry around. Just remember to file your notes so that you can review them later, like for a final exam or a future course. Use a folder or an accordion filing system to keep old notes organized.

Stick to plain paper
Some people prefer lined paper, others blank. Try both and see what works for you. The best type of paper for taking notes is plain white paper. Your notes will show up clearer on plain, rather than colored paper.

Taking good study notes

When taking study notes remember to write down just the main points of what is being said, and write it in whatever way you will be most likely to remember. These are your study notes, so there is no wrong way, if you understand it. We will go into quite a bit more detail about taking notes soon.

Dating and labeling your notes

Get into the habit of writing the date and subject of your class on all your notes. It's critical for good organization and finding what you need later.

Write in your own words

When writing notes, don't worry about copying exactly what your teacher says. It's best to write your notes in your own words. They will be easier for you to study from.

Write clearly

The most important habit you can get into when taking notes in class it to write clearly – or clearly enough anyway. Notes don't have to be masterpieces, but you have to be able to read them. If you can't read what you've written, they aren't going to be much help. You don't want to waste your time re-writing all your class notes.

Don't use a laptop

Unless you're an exceptionally fast touch typist who can structure notes effectively while typing and listening, this is probably not a great strategy. Laptops or handheld devices offer any number of potential distractions, like the temptation to go online, chat with friends, etc. It's best to turn off all electronic devices and keep your full focus on the class.

Don't waste time repeating facts

You don't have to bother writing the same facts over and over again in your notes, even if your teacher tends to repeat a point. If the teacher repeats something, that is a sure sign it is important, but you don't have to write it down again - try underlining. Make sure you write as much down as you can, even if you feel like you understand it. You don't want to have to rely on your memory when it comes time for a test. It's best to have the facts down in your study notes so they can be reviewed, or clarified later.

Don't worry about complete sentences

Don't worry about sentence structure or punctuation. Jot notes in list or point form, with bullets, or in number form. Facts are easiest to study if they are listed in point form. Don't try to write in paragraphs - you won't have time and will miss too much while trying to formulate paragraphs.

Listen for hints

Keep your ears open for any hints on possible test questions. Many times a teacher will comment on the importance of information and infer, or actually say that the information will appear on an upcoming test. Make sure you highlight the information the instructor tells you is important. Take notes on any comments the teacher says about the material. She might indicate some material is more important than others, and some should be memorized sooner than others.

Find what works for you

Find a style of note taking that works best for you. It doesn't matter if no one else can decipher what your abbreviations stand for, or what symbols mean. As long as you can remember what it means, then your study notes are doing the trick.

Look over your notes regularly

It's a good idea to read over your notes regularly, preferably within 24 hours and then on a regular schedule after that. Studies show this improves your retention and understanding of the material by a huge amount. If you put notes away until the end of the term, when you have to review for an exam, you might forget some of the details of a lesson from your notes alone. By regularly reviewing notes you can keep the main points fresh in your mind.

It's also a good idea to leave space at the end of your notes so you can add more material when it's time for review. See the Split Page and Cornell methods described below.

Organize your notes

Get in the habit of writing more detailed study notes from your class notes. You can elaborate on points made in a lecture when you've got more time, remembering to underline the main topic discussed in the class, as well as the sub-topics, and the key words. See the Cornell and Split Page methods below.

Extra reading

It's worth it to do a little extra reading in a subject. Your study notes will have more meaning if you read more on the subject. You can elaborate on what you have learned in class and it will not only allow you to do well in class, but also carry on into your future education.

Giving yourself clues

With practice you will become more skilled taking notes and will be able to write effective clues in your notes that will jog your memory to key facts and concepts. Study clues work as reminders to trigger a whole set of information. With practice you will know which clues work best for you.

•

Method 1 - Outline Method

The outline method of note taking is one that will probably look familiar.

The outline method starts on the left-hand side of the paper. The most important points are placed at the left edge of the paper. Less important points, which are usually ideas that support the main points, are indented to the right. Each set of less important points is indented more to the right. It is easy to see, at a glance, how importance the different ideas because of the distance between them and the major points is greater.

An alternative, which is more difficult and requires a little more thought, is to start with minor points to the left and indent as the points get more important. This alternate outline form is best used in lectures where minor ideas are used to build up to the most important ideas.

With either form, indentation is enough to show the importance of the ideas and the relationship between them. Variations include using dashes, bullets or Roman numerals and letters.

It doesn't matter how you organize your notes. The important point is to always use the same ordering system.

Speed is key when taking notes, and using complicated numbering systems will slow you down. You may want to consider adding the marks after class when you review your notes.

An Outline looks something like this:

I. First main topic

   A. Subtopic

      1. Detail
      2. Detail

   B. Subtopic

II. Second main topic
   A. Subtopic

ADVANTAGES AND DISADVANTAGES OF THE OUTLINE METHOD

ADVANTAGES

Outlining shows the content and main points of the lecture, but also the relationship between the points. With an outline, it is easy to see the main points, and reviewing your notes is easy. The outline is easy to learn and notes using the Outline Method can be easily understood.

A major benefit of the outline method is the ability to focus on the lecture. Outlining is simple and fast so you can concentrate on the lecture.

DISADVANTAGES

The Outline Method can be difficult to use in science and math courses. Courses with fast-paced lectures may also be difficult to outline, partially because outlining requires the note-taker to think about organization.

THE CORNELL METHOD

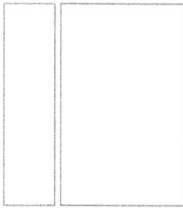

The first step to using the Cornell method is to divide your paper into three sections. Approximately 2 inches from the bottom of your paper, draw a horizontal line all the way across the page.

Approximately 2.5 inches from the left side of your paper, draw a vertical line from the top to the horizontal line you have just drawn. On standard paper, this will give you a 2.5 x 9-inch section on the left, a 6 x 9-inch section on the right, and a 2 x 8.5-inch section at the bottom. It is important that you create all three sections because each section has its own purpose in the Cornell method.

Once you have divided your paper into three sections, you are ready to take notes. The 6 x 9-inch section is your note-taking section. This is where you begin the six R's of note taking.

Free Cornell Method Template

https://www.test-preparation.ca/pdf/Cornell-Method-Template.pdf

1. Record – During the lecture, record your notes in the note-taking section. Just capture the main points. Grammar, punctuation and spelling are not vital, if you can read your notes later. You may want to develop your own shorthand or abbreviation method for your notes. Just be sure you can remember and understand them once you've left the classroom.

2. Reduce – After the lecture, reduce your notes to main keywords. These are cues to help you remember the information, and they are written in the 2.5-inch section to the left of the notes. The cue section is also a good place to note any questions that you have as you go over your notes.

3. Summarize – The summary of your notes goes in the 2-inch space at the bottom of the page. Summarize each page of notes at the bottom of that page. You can also summarize the entire lecture on the last page of the notes for that lecture. Most lists place recapitulation as the last step in the 6 R's, but it is best to write your summary after you write your cues in the left-hand column. Writing it immediately ensures that the information is still fresh in your mind, which helps you create a more accurate summary.

4. Say it Back – Actually saying it out loud can help to reinforce the learning process. Ideally, you can cover up the note-taking section and use the cue section to jog your memory when reciting.

5. Reflect – Think about your notes and the information that you have just learned. Consider how the information can be applied, and how it fits with what you already know. Figure out the significance of the information, and why knowing it is important.

6. Review – Review your notes frequently to keep from forgetting the information. If you set aside time several days each week to review and recite your notes, you will not have to worry about an all-night cram session before the exam.

ADVANTAGES OF THE CORNELL METHOD

The Cornell Method can be used for any subject. The Cornell Method is an organized and systematic way to take and review notes.

The format makes it easy to pulling out major concepts

and ideas.

The Cornell Method is simple and efficient saving time and effort.

The Cornell Method is a "Do-it-right-in-the-first-place" system.

DISADVANTAGES OF THE CORNELL METHOD

The Cornell Method requires special paper.
The Cornell Method takes some time to learn.

SPLIT-PAGE METHOD

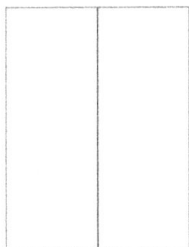

The split-page method is exactly what it sounds like. You split the page by drawing a vertical line all the way down the paper. The line should be located 2.5 to 3 inches from the left-hand side of the paper.

Free Split Page Template

https://www.test-preparation.ca/pdf/Split-Page-Method-Template.pdf

So, what do you do with the two sides?

Similar to the Cornell method, the split-page method uses the right side of the divided page for recording lecture notes.

The left-hand side of the page can have one of two uses. Some students prefer to use the left column for writing down keywords from the notes or questions they may have about the material. This allows them to cover the notes and use only the keywords as prompts when reciting the information. If you use the left-hand column for cues and keywords, be sure to write them down as soon as possible after the lecture, while the information is still fresh in your mind.

The more traditional use for the left side is creating an outline of the textbook by writing down keywords and main points, also known as the Outline method of taking notes. The trick to this method is to keep the information from the textbook and the notes together, and to separate chapters. With this format, a student is able to study the textbook and the lecture notes side-by-side, without wasting time or losing their train of thought by flipping back and forth between notes and textbook.

A variation of the split-page method is to divide the page into three columns. The middle column is used for taking notes in class. The left-hand column is used for outlining the text. The right-hand column is used for writing down keywords, cues, and questions the student may have. This format provides the text-book and notes in one location, and has the bonus of a cue column. This allows students to cover the first two columns and use the cues in the third column as memory prompts when reciting the information.

ADVANTAGES OF THE SPLIT PAGE METHOD

The Split Page Method is simple and easy and makes picking out the main ideas fast. The Split Page Method is easier to use than the Cornell Method.

Like the Cornell Method, it can be used for any subject.

DISADVANTAGES OF THE SPLIT PAGE METHOD

None

CHARTING METHOD

Charting is where you create a table with rows and columns to show information and the relationship between facts. Mapping is a picture of the ideas. The Outline method used one sentence on a separate line for each idea and the notes are like a table of contents or index.

Main Idea	Main Idea	Main Idea
Point 1	Point 1	Point 1
Point 2	Point 2	Point 2
Point 3	Point 3	Point 3
Point 4	Point 4	Point 4

MAPPING METHOD

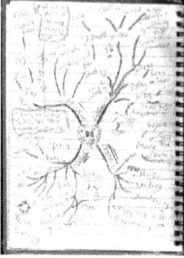

The traditional way to take notes is to write down the main concepts and sub topics as quickly as possible during a lecture and then make corrections later to fill in any gaps.

The problem with this process is it doesn't really involve any thinking – it is just a straight copying down. Notes don't record the connections between the ideas.

Mind mapping is a note taking technique where words, ideas, are linked to and arranged around a keyword or idea. Mind mapping allows you to see, structure and classify ideas, quickly and easily.

Compared to other note taking methods, mind mapping generally takes less space and it claims to be a better method for learning and remembering what you have learned.

5 METHODS FOR TAKING NOTES

Below are 3 sample lectures with notes in each of the five styles described above.

What is a QR Code? A QR code looks like a barcode and it's used as a shortcut to link to content online using your phone's camera, saving you from typing lengthy addresses into your mobile browser.

Here is a recommended practice method:

Read Passage #1 and review the different styles until you are very familiar with each.

For Passages #2 and #3, listen to the audio files and take notes in each of the 5 styles.

This will give you lots of practice and familiarize with how each style works for you.

After this practice you should be able to choose the best style for you, or make your own composite style.

TAKING NOTES PRACTICE

PASSAGE #1 - CLOUDS

Scan QR or go to

https://www.test-preparation.ca/audio/Lectures/Clouds.wav

Clouds are divided into two categories, stratus clouds (or stratiform, the Latin stratus meaning layer) and cumulus clouds (or cumuliform; cumulus means piled up).

These two cloud types are divided into 3 more groups according to the cloud's altitude or height, High, Middle and Low.

High clouds

These generally form above 16,500 feet (5,000 m), in the troposphere. The prefix cirro- or cirrus is used on all high cloud names. At this height, water freezes so clouds are made of ice crystals. High clouds tend to be wispy, and are often see through.

High Clouds include:

* Cirrus
* Cirrostratus
* Cirrocumulus

Middle clouds

These clouds develop between 6,500 and 16,500 feet (between 2,000 and 5,000 m). The prefix alto- is used on all middle clouds. These clouds are made of water droplets.

Middle Clouds include:

* Altostratus
* Altocumulus

Low Clouds

Low clouds are found up to 6,500 feet (2,000 m) and include the stratus (dense and grey). When stratus clouds contact the ground, they are called fog.

Low Clouds include:

* Stratus
* Nimbostratus
* Stratocumulus

OUTLINE METHOD - PASSAGE 1

1. Clouds
     A. 2 categories stratus and cumulus. 3 more
groups by height, High, Middle, and Low.
B.   High Clouds

          1. above 16,500 feet
          2. prefix cirro-
          3. made of ice
          4. wispy
          5. cirrus, cirrostratus, cirroculus

C. Middle Clouds

          1. 6,600 – 16,500 ft.
          2. prefix alto-
          3. made of water drops
          4. altostratus, altocumulus

     D. Low Clouds

          1. up to 6,500 ft.
          2. stratus, nimbostratus, stratocumulus

CORNELL METHOD - PASSAGE 1

2 categories stratus and cumulus. 3 more groups by height, High, Middle, and Low.

High Clouds
above 16,500 ft
prefix cirro-
made of ice
wispy
cirrus, cirrostratus, cirrocumulus

Middle Clouds
6,600 – 16,500 ft.
prefix alto-
made of water drops
altostratus, altocumulus

Low Clouds
up to 6,500 ft.
stratus, nimbostratus, stratocumulus

2 categories, stratus clouds cumulus clouds 4 groups High, Middle and Low.

High
These generally form above 16,500 feet (5,000 m), in the troposphere. The prefix cirro- or cirrus is used on all high cloud names. water freezes ice crystals. High clouds see through. Cirrus, Cirrostratus and Cirrocumulus.

Middle
6,500 and 16,500 feet made of water droplets. Altostratus and Altocumulus.

Low
up to 6,500 fee t dense grey On Ground - fog. Stratus, Nimbostratus and Stratocumulus.

3 types of clouds by height - High above 16,500 ft ,prefix cirro- made of ice
wispy cirrus, cirrostratus, cirrocumulus. Middle 6,600 – 16,500 ft. alto- water drops, altostratus, altocumulus. Low up to 6,500 ft.
stratus, nimbostratus, stratocumulus

SPLIT PAGE METHOD - PASSAGE 1

2 categories stratus and cumulus. 3 more groups by height, High, Middle, and Low.	2 categories, stratus clouds cumulus clouds 4 groups High, Middle and Low.
High Clouds above 16,500 ft prefix cirro- made of ice wispy cirrus, cirrostratus, cirrocumulus	High These generally form above 16,500 feet (5,000 m), in the troposphere. The prefix cirro- or cirrus is used on all high cloud names. water freezes ice crystals. High clouds see through. Cirrus, Cirrostratus and Cirrocumulus.
Middle Clouds 6,600 – 16,500 ft. prefix alto- made of water drops altostratus, altocumulus	Middle 6,500 and 16,500 feet made of water droplets. Altostratus and Altocumulus.
Low Clouds up to 6,500 ft. stratus, nimbostratus, stratocumulus	Low up to 6,500 fee t dense grey On Ground - fog. Stratus, Nimbostratus and Stratocumulus.

MAPPING METHOD - PASSAGE 1
Clouds

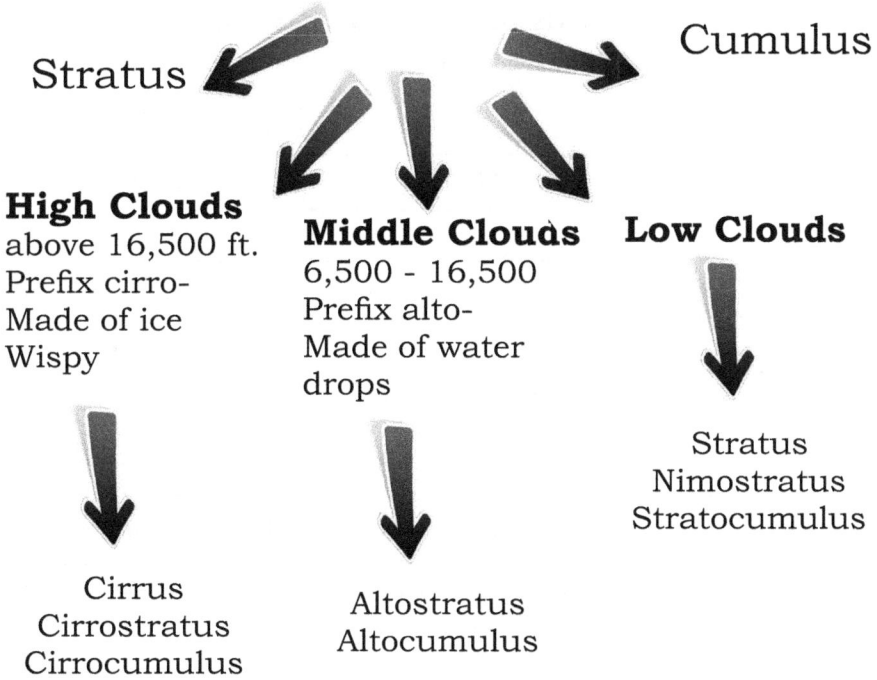

Stratus

Cumulus

High Clouds
above 16,500 ft.
Prefix cirro-
Made of ice
Wispy

Middle Clouds
6,500 - 16,500
Prefix alto-
Made of water
drops

Low Clouds

Stratus
Nimostratus
Stratocumulus

Cirrus
Cirrostratus
Cirrocumulus

Altostratus
Altocumulus

CHARTING METHOD - PASSAGE 1

2 Categories – Stratus and Cumulus 3 more groups,
by height, High, Middle, Low

High	Middle	Low
Above 16,500 ft	6500- 16,500 ft.	Up to 6,500 ft
Prefix cirro-	Prefix alto-	
Made of ice	Made of water drops	
Cirruc Cirrostratus Cirrocumulus	Altostratus Altocumulus	Stratus Nimbostratus Stratocumulus

SAMPLE PASSAGE #2

Scan QR or go to
https://www.test-preparation.ca/audio/Lectures/Planets4.wav

A planet is a large round mass in orbit around a star.

The name comes from the Greek term planētēs, meaning "wanderer," as ancient astronomers noted how lights moved across the sky.

The International Astronomical Union lists eight planets in our solar system. The planets in our system are Mercury, Venus, Earth, Mars, Jupiter, Saturn, Uranus, and Neptune.

The word "planet" does not have a precise scientific definition, and so many astronomers argue that Pluto should be removed from the list while others argue the number of planets should be raised to ten or even higher depending on how planets are defined.

The International Astronomical Union, after much debate, recently decided Pluto is not a planet.

A large round object was found between Mars and Jupiter, named Ceres, which was called a planet at first, but later classified as an asteroid.

Many large round objects have been seen beyond Neptune, including Sedna, but they have not been recognized as planets by the International Astronomical Union.

OUTLINING METHOD - PASSAGE #2

1. Planet
   a. Comes From Greek word, Planetes, or wanderer.
   b. Large, round mass and orbits around a star.
   c. Nine planets in our solar system.
      1. Mercury
      2. Venus
      3. Earth
      4. Mars
      5. Jupiter
      6. Saturn
      7. Uranus
      8. Neptune
         No precise scientific definition.

2. International Astronomical Union
   a. Lists Planets in our solar system.
   b. Expected to define planets better
   c. Decided Pluto is not a planet

3. Non-Planets
   a. Ceres - Between Mars and Jupiter
   b. Sedna - Past Neptune

CORNELL METHOD - PASSAGE 2

Planet- From Greek, Planetes, = wanderer No precise scientific definition Large, round mass that orbits a star. 9 planets in solar system - Mercury, Venus, Earth, Mars, Jupiter, Saturn, Uranus, Neptune Int. Astronomical Union Will define planets better Decided - Pluto not a planet Non-Planets Ceres Between Mars & Jupiter Sedna - Past Neptune	Planet - from Greek Planetes, or wanderer No precise scientific def. Lge, round mass orbits star 9 planets - Mercury, Venus, Earth, Mars, Jupiter, Saturn, Uranus, Neptune Int. Astronomical Union - decides IAU will define planets better IAU decided Pluto not planet Non-Planets in S. System Ceres - Mars - Jupiter Sedna - Past Neptune

9 planets in solar - Mercury, Venus, Earth, Mars, Jupiter, Saturn, Uranus, Neptune

Planet (Greek, Planetes, = wanderer) large round mass orbiting - no precise def. Int. Astronomical Union - decides - Will define planets better

IAU Decided - Pluto not a planet

Non-Planets in S. system - Ceres Between Mars & Jupiter & Sedna - Past Neptune

SPLIT PAGE METHOD - PASSAGE 2

Planet - from Greek Planetes, or wanderer No precise scientific def. Lge, round mass orbits star 9 planets - Mercury, Venus, Earth, Mars, Jupiter, Saturn, Uranus, Neptune Int. Astronomical Union - decides IAU will define planets better IAU decided Pluto not planet Non-Planets in S. System Ceres - Mars - Jupiter Sedna - Past Neptune	Planet - from Greek Planetes, or wanderer No precise scientific def. Lge, round mass orbits star 9 planets - Mercury, Venus, Earth, Mars, Jupiter, Saturn, Uranus, Neptune Int. Astronomical Union - decides IAU will define planets better IAU decided Pluto not planet Non-Planets in S. System Ceres - Mars - Jupiter Sedna - Past Neptune

CHARTING METHOD - PASSAGE #2

Planets: Large round mass that orbits around a star; 9 listed in our system, comes from Greek word "Planetes" meaning wanderer.

Planets	Non-Planets	International Astronomical Union
Mercury Earth Venus Mars Jupiter Saturn Uranus Neptune	Ceres	Lists Planets In our Solar system
	Sedna	Decided Pluto is not a planet

MAPPING METHOD - PASSAGE #2

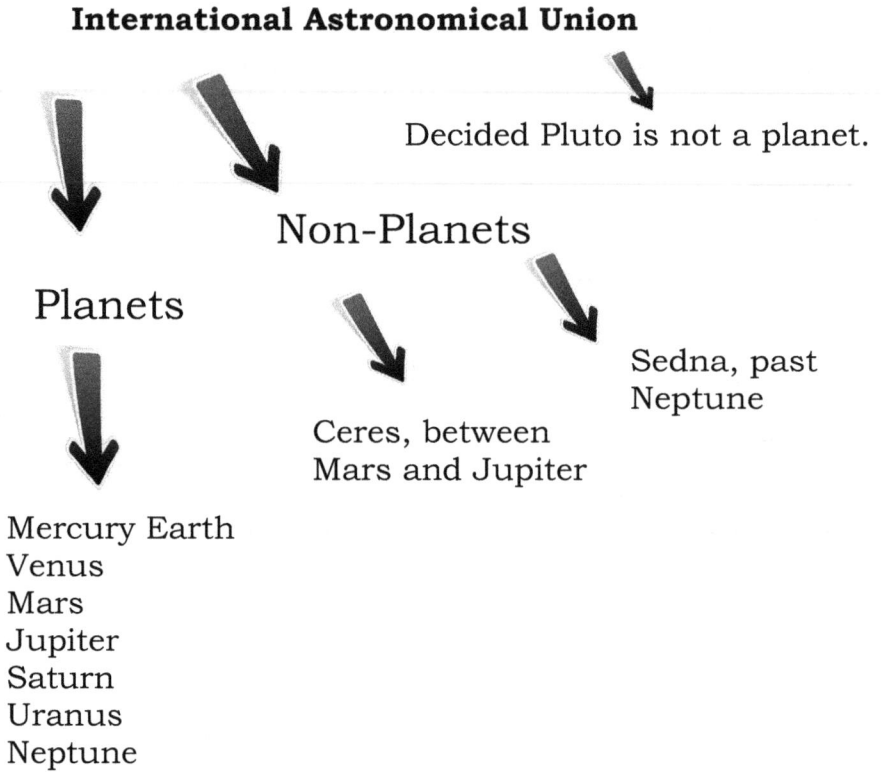

International Astronomical Union

Decided Pluto is not a planet.

Non-Planets

Planets

Ceres, between
Mars and Jupiter

Sedna, past
Neptune

Mercury Earth
Venus
Mars
Jupiter
Saturn
Uranus
Neptune

SAMPLE PASSAGE #3 - THE SOLAR SYSTEM

Scan QR or go to
https://www.test-preparation.ca/audio/Lectures/SolarSystem.wav

The Solar System is made up of the Sun and other celestial (outer space) objects, which rotate around the sun and are held in place by gravity.

These celestial objects can be broken into three categories, the eight planets and their 166 moons, three dwarf planets. In addition there are billions of small bodies such as asteroids, comets, meteoroids, interplanetary dust, and Kuiper belt objects.

Beyond the Kuiper belt is the scattered disc, the heliopause, and finally the hypothetical Oort cloud, which is outside the solar system.

The eight plants, in order from the closest to the furthest from the Sun are, Mercury (the closest), Venus, Earth, Mars, Jupiter, Saturn, Uranus, and Neptune, the furthest from the sun. There are two types of planets, terrestrial and four gas giants.

The three dwarf planets are Ceres, Pluto, and Eris as well as their four moons.

Six of these planets have moons "natural satellites," termed after Earth's Moon. Each outer planet has planetary rings of dust. Every planet but Earth is named after the gods and goddesses from Greco-Roman mythology.

The three dwarf planets consist of the following:

1. Pluto, the largest known Kuiper belt object
2. Ceres, the largest object in the steroid belt
3. Eris, the largest of the three, which lies in the scattered disk.

OUTLINING METHOD - PASSAGE #3

1. The Solar System
   a. Contains Sun & celestial objects
   b. Celestial objects
      1. The Sun
      2. Eight planets – Terrestrial & Gas Giants
      3. 3 dwarf planets
      4. billions smaller objects
         1. asteroids
         2. comets
         3. meteors
         4. dust
         5. Kuiper belt objects

2. Celestial objects - 4 categories

    a. Planets Eight Planets & 166 moons

        1. Mercury
        2. Venus
        3. Earth
        4. Mars
        5. Jupiter
        6. Saturn
        7. Uranus
        8. Neptune

    b. Three Dwarf Planets & 4 moons

        1. Ceres
        2. Pluto
        3. Eris

    c. Billions small bodies

        1.   Asteroids
        2.   Meteors

    3. Named after Greek gods, goddesses (except Earth)

CORNELL METHOD - PASSAGE #3

Sun 8 planets 3 dwarf small obj. 4 Categories of Celestial obj. 8 Planets Moons Mercury, Ve- nus, Earth, Mars, Jupi- ter, Saturn, Uranus, Neptune Asteroids Meteors	The Solar System - Contains Sun & celestial obj. Sun & 8 planets – Terrestrial & Gas Giants + 3 dwarf planets billions smaller objects - incl. asteroids, comets, meteors, dust, Kuiper belt objects Celestial objects - 4 cat. Planets - 8 Planets & 166 moons - Mercury, Venus, Earth, Mars, Ju- piter, Saturn, Uranus, Neptune 3 Dwarf Planets & moons - Ceres, Pluto, Eris Billions - Asteroids & Meteors

Solar System is made of Sun + 8 planets & 3 dwarf
Planets
small obj - Asteroids & Meteors

SPLIT PAGE METHOD - PASSAGE #3

Sun 8 planets 3 dwarf small obj. 4 Categories of Celestial obj. 8 Planets Moons Mercury, Venus, Earth, Mars, Jupiter, Saturn, Uranus, Neptune Asteroids Meteors	The Solar System - Contains Sun & celestial obj. Sun & 8 planets – Terrestrial & Gas Giants + 3 dwarf planets billions smaller objects - incl. asteroids, comets, meteors, dust, Kuiper belt objects Celestial objects - 4 cat. Planets - 8 Planets & 166 moons - Mercury, Venus, Earth, Mars, Jupiter, Saturn, Uranus, Neptune 3 Dwarf Planets & moons - Ceres, Pluto, Eris Billions - Asteroids & Meteors

CHARTING METHOD - PASSAGE #3

Solar System: 3 categories of celestial objects, 8 planets + moons, 3 dwarf planets + moons, and smaller bodies.

8 Planets	Three Dwarf Planets	Small Bodies
Mercury	Pluto	Asteroids
Venus	Eris	meteorites
Earth	Ceres	Other small objects
Mars		
Jupiter		
Saturn		
Uranus		
Neptune		
Named after Greek Gods/ Goddesses		

MAPPING METHOD - PASSAGE #3

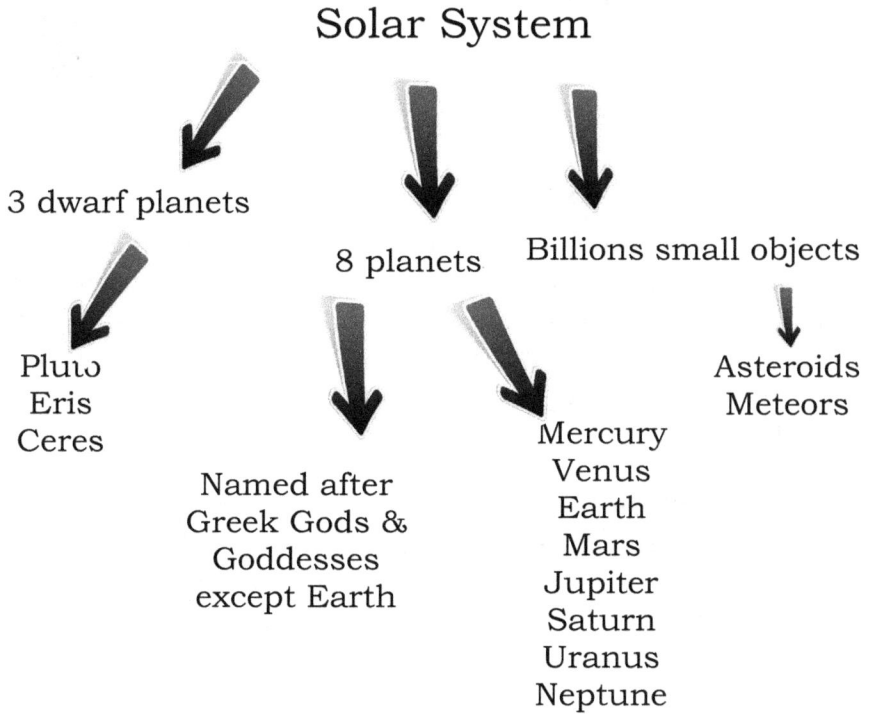

Solar System

3 dwarf planets

8 planets

Billions small objects

Pluto
Eris
Ceres

Named after
Greek Gods &
Goddesses
except Earth

Mercury
Venus
Earth
Mars
Jupiter
Saturn
Uranus
Neptune

Asteroids
Meteors

PASSAGE #4 -
CATERPILLARS

https://www.test-preparation.ca/audio/Caterpillar-2.mp3

Butterflies and moths have a three stage life cycle.
Caterpillars are the first or laval stage. Caterpillars can be
either herbivores, feeding mostly on plants, or carnivores,
feeding on other insects. Caterpillars eat continuously.
Once they are too big for their body, they shed or molt
their skin.

Some caterpillars have symbiotic relationships with other
insects. A symbiotic relationship is where different species
work together in a way that is either harmful or helpful.
Symbiotic relationships are critical to many species and
ecosystems.

Some caterpillars and ants have a symbiotic or mutual
relationship where both benefit. Ants give some protection,
and caterpillars provide the ants with honeydew nectar.

Ants and caterpillars communicate by vibrations through
the soil as well as grunting and squeaking. Humans are

not able to hear these communications.

Passage #5 - Gardens

https://www.test-preparation.ca/audio/Gardens-2.mp3

Roman gardens were initially built to supply the household with vegetables and herbs. Later, the influence from Greek and Persian gardens changed Roman gardens to pleasure gardens in palaces and villas, as well as public parks meant for enjoyment and exercise. At this time Roman gardens had their famous statues and sculptures.

Later with the fall of the Roman Empire, gardening declined and during the Middle Ages, gardening was strictly for herbs used in various medicines, and for decorating churches.

Persian garden were surrounded by walls and meant to look like paradise. Traditional Islamic gardens are heavily influence by the desert, an important part of Persian culture. Therefore, water and shade are important elements. Gardens, in Islamic culture, are for meditation and rest. Sunlight is an important feature of Persian gardens and often the architecture, layout and textures highlight reflected sunlight. Persian gardens are built on an indoor/outdoor plan that often uses courtyards.

PASSAGE #6 - INSECT PESTS

www.test-preparation.ca/audio/InsectPests-2.mp3

A pest is an organism that is destructive to crops, humans, structures, or other animals. Insect pests make up about 1% of the insect family. Many insects such as bees and silkworms are beneficial.

Many blood-sucking insects carry diseases the pick up from infected hosts and pass on.

Some insects that were previously harmless, can become pests if they are introduced to a new area. In the new area often insects do not have natural predators.

Often insects carry diseases. The common housefly breeds on organic wastes and can carry diseases to food which is consumed by humans.

Pests can be controlled using insecticides and introducing natural predators. For example, farmers introduce predators such as ladybugs to their crops to control various insect pests.

PASSAGE #8 - FLAME

https://www.test-preparation.ca/audio/Flame-2.mp3

Flames are the visible gaseous part of the fire. Flames have a wide range of colors and temperatures, which depends on the type of fuel. Fire continues to burn in a chain reaction that feeds on itself. The heat from the fire reaction vaporizes fuel molecules, which react with oxygen, creating more heat.

Incomplete combustion, generally of organic matter, produces an orange flame, releases less energy and produces carbon monoxide which is a poisonous gas.

When the combustion of a gas is complete the flame is blue.

The color of the flame, as well as the temperature, and therefore the rate of combustion depend on the fuel and oxygen supply mix.

Many combustion reactions do not require a flame, such as the reaction in an internal combustion engine. Various ways are used to eliminate a flame in combustion engines depending on the type of fuel.

TIPS FOR TAKING NOTES

➡ Put the name of the class at the top of the page.

➡ Put the date at the top of the page.

➡ Put the page # at the top of the page.

➡ Write down the basic topic of the lecture.

➡ Use 8 ½" by 11" paper in a loose-leaf binder.

➡ Take notes in pen.

➡ Make sure you can read your notes! They don't have to be super neat but you do have to read them.

➡ Keep all your notes for each class together. Use separators with color tabs to divide your notes for each subject.

➡ Always copy all information from the chalkboard or overhead transparencies.

➡ Review your notes as soon as possible after class, to fill in the gaps for information that you missed. Do this while the lecture is still fresh in your mind.

➡ If you miss class, get notes from another student.

COMMON ABBREVIATIONS & SYMBOLS FOR TAKING NOTES

If you are taking notes while someone is speaking, then you are going to have to write fast!

Writing fast means taking every short cut you can. Below are a list of common abbreviations and symbols.

e.g.	for example
i.e.	that is
etc.	etcetera: and so on
c.f.	compare
viz.	namely
c.(or ca.)	about/approximately
N.B.	note
C19	nineteenth century; similarly C20 etc.
1920s	i.e. 1920-1929; similarly 1970s etc.
approx.	approximately
dept	department
diff.(s)	difficult(y)(-ies)
excl.	excluding
govt.	government
imp.	important/importance
incl.	including
info.	information
lang.	language
ltd	limited
max.	maximum
min.	minimum
1st	first
2nd	second
3rd	third etc.

G.B.	Great Britain
U.K.	United Kingdom
Eng.	English
Brit.	British
Q.	question
A.	answer
p./pp.	page/pages
poss.	possible/possibly
prob.	probable/probably
probs.	problems
re-	with reference to/concerning
ref.	reference
sts	students
tho'	though
thro'	through
v.	very
s/t	something
s/o	someone
÷	statement/answer is correct
x	statement/answer is wrong
?	question; is the statement correct?
/	or (this/that = this or that)
& or +	and/plus
-	a dash (often used to join ideas and replace words or punctuation marks that have been omitted)
" "	ditto (means the same as the words immediately above the ditto marks)
≠	does not equal, differs from, is the opposite of
=	is/are/have/has/equals
Æ	leads to/results in/causes
SYMBOL	MEANING
&	and

@	at
/	per
↑	increasing, increased, increases, rises
↓	decreasing, decreased, decreases, falls
=	equal to, is
≠	not equal to, is not
w/	with
w/o	without
w/i	within
etc.	et cetera, so forth
b/4	before
b/c	because
esp.	especially
diff.	difference
min.	minimum
max.	maximum
gov't	goverment
ex.	example
2	to, two, too

How to Study from your Notes

Do you take notes during class lectures and never seem to look at the notes again? If you are filing your class notes away, and not using the valuable information found in your notes, you may be missing a key study tool. Notes are a vital part of your success when preparing for a test, as they are one of the best sources of information you have. Using your class lecture notes may not be as intuitive as reading the textbook, but once you learn how to study from your lecture notes, you'll learn more quickly.

Get Organized

The first step to successfully study from your notes is to take organized notes! Taking notes can seem tedious and frustrating if you don't know what you are doing. However, with the methods we've provided you will have well-organized notes that will be a breeze to study from.

This means more than just mindlessly jotting down every word you listen to or read. Taking notes helps you remember. You have to actively decide what information is key and write it down.

The key to good note taking is organization. Being organized enables you to effectively use the written information and memorize it. Your notes should be simple, but include some key phrases or vocabulary that will stick in your memory, so that you can recall the full information when you look back. Aside from these terms, keep the notes in your own words. This will help you understand the content more easily. Most importantly, only write down what is important.

You may find it easier to take notes on your computer. If you decide to take your computer to class and type your notes, look for a note taking program with simple interface that will allow you to concentrate on your note taking and not on the other programs your computer can run. Keep in mind that typing up notes are good for fast paced lectures, but also leave you mindless while inputting the information.

Whatever note taking method you determine is ideal for you, use paper notes when it is time to study. Collect your notes and use them to clarify the information you are reading and studying. Paper notes are useful when studying because you can write additional information on the paper and even highlight information that you do not understand. You can then return to your class and gain additional information to fill in your notes.

To succeed on a test, you must take complete notes! If you only have incomplete notes written down about the topic, then you will only partially understand the material, and not be fully prepared for a test. Students often won't use the classroom notes because they believe they are incomplete. There are many ways to fill in these blanks or to check your notes.

Often in college, the professors will have the classroom notes written on a PowerPoint and posted to the class website. Check to see if that is true for your situation. If so, this is a valuable resource that you can come back to again and again. If this isn't the case, then check with your teacher to see if they offer the notes or would be willing to discuss the important topics details should have written.

Check the material you've been given in class. Use any handouts, homework, or the textbook to write down key information, which will come up again when it's time to study.

If you feel you are missing key information in your class notes, join a study group and help each other fill in the missing blanks. You could also simply check-in with your classmates to compare what you both have written. As it gets closer to the exam, you can exchange the information you have and study together. You may also want to rewrite your notes after class and fill in the missing information while it is fresh in your mind.

Incorporating your classroom notes into your study sessions can help you to learn more information in a quicker manner. Reading your textbook will be easier if you use your class lecture notes to guide your reading and refresh your memory during the first part of your study session. Your classroom notes can be a helpful tool to your entire learning process, stop filing the information away and start using them.

Completely rereading your textbook or classroom material can waste time while studying, especially if you have to cram. Use your notes to study from and your textbook to supplement that information. By using the notes you took during the previous lessons and readings, you will save yourself time and frustration. Use the notes to create study questions and quiz yourself. This will help you determine which areas you are strong in and where you may need to go back and study more.

Your notes might also have information that your teacher or professor said would be on the test, but isn't in your textbook or any of the class handouts. Sometimes teachers will feel generous and give a preview or a full question that is on the test as a bonus. This can be extremely helpful in getting you that A, so you want to make sure you have everything written correctly in your notes.

Reduce and rewrite your notes. Normally when taking, you are trying to listen to all the information while frantically scribbling it down. If you have the time, go through all your written work and redo it. Not only will you be reading through the information again and further implementing it into your hand's memory, but you will also be able to determine what is important. You can weed out any fluff that will distract you from the real content, and add in anything that you may have missed. Although it can be time consuming, you will be thanking yourself when it comes time to study and you have detailed notes that you can actually read.

Repeat and reflect upon the information. As you study, try reading the material out loud and in your own words. You will find that you can actively recall more of the information afterwards, but can also find out any spaces in your comprehension that you can work on. Reflection allows you to think about the information at a deeper level, and encourages you to make connections. This act is beneficial because you are more likely to remember something you are personally linked with. Ask questions that you may have and see if you can answer them or bring them up during class time, so that there can be a larger discussion.

Overall, you want to try and connect with your notes in a variety of different ways, which will utilize different learning paths and keep you engaged in the process!

How to Study from Textbooks

The reading of textbooks is an integral and unavoidable part of your college education. Although in the classroom a teacher may cover much of the content of the subject matter, many of the details of the topic will be fleshed out from your textbook. Unfortunately much of the material you will encounter in a textbook can be dry, making it difficult to stay focused and study. Concentration is essential to your success in the class.

All the material you are required to learn is crucial for your success. Especially at a collegiate level, professors don't just assign busy work, so everything you read has a meaning. The readings in a textbook will show up throughout the course in homework, class discussions, tests, and projects, so it is up to you to have a thorough understanding to contribute to the conversation. At this upper level of education, some of the readings can be dense and difficult to understand, which is why you need to create methods to tackle these texts in an efficient manner.

A Systematic Method for Study-ing Textbooks

To get the essential information from your textbook it is important to follow a systematic process. This will help you retain more of what you read and build a solid base of knowledge, which in turn will make it easier to study for the next test. We've provided you with a process along with other methods, for you to maximize your studying time and thoroughly learn the material.

1) Begin by reviewing the title and headers of the chapter you are reading.

If you are following instructions to build something, you will most likely review all the instructions first before beginning. This preview allows you to get a sense of what you will encounter and how that material will progress through the textbook.

This is called Surveying. Surveying gives you an overview of what you are about to delve into and lets you familiarize yourself with the main concepts. With this action, you can prepare an outline or flow of the materials you are about to cover in your reading. It allows your mind to organize and prepare for the subject matter. In addition to the titles, also read the graphs, pictures, etc. to immerse yourself in the text.

2) Convert the chapter headings or main ideas into questions.

Ask yourself who, what, when, where, why or how. Write these questions down. This allows you to focus in on what you are reading and gives you purpose, so that you are not aimlessly reading. Once you've read through a section, highlight of a couple pieces that sums up the main ideas or seem important. Don't overdo the highlighting, as you should be able to read the key parts quickly without going over the whole paragraph. Use your notes or the margins of the text to write in questions that could be answered by the highlighted information.

As tempting as it may be, don't take notes or highlight while you are reading through the text for the first time. This action can not only distract you from the material, but unless you've read the whole text, you won't know which parts are important enough to high-light.

3) Note any additional subheadings with questions.

After you've finished reading the chapter, go back to your paper and make sure all of your written questions have been answered in a complete manner. Make sure there are no other questions that come to mind that need answering.

As important as it is to have a full understanding of the material, you should keep your responses to the questions concise. Otherwise, you might as well be reading the exact text.

Don't forget to pay attention to any tables, charts, and photographs that are mentioned in the textbook. There is often additional information set aside in boxes on the pages that add to what is written in the body of the text. Take care to note or highlight this information as well as they are usually important.

4) Finally, review the summary of the chapter and complete the questions at the end of the chapter.

Use your notes to complete the answers, and write down any questions you didn't find in your own notes. As you go back through the chapter underline the proper heading to locate these unanswered questions and write them on your paper along with the question.

Ultimately, after finishing the reading you should be able to answer the questions you wrote down. If you do happen to struggle with them, then you can just check the highlighted portions. Keeping a written question and answer format of your textbook reading will help you when you are involved in classroom discussion. It will allow you to probe your teacher for any answers that weren't clear to you during the reading, and will make studying for your test that much easier.

You should also write other questions or observations, so you can bring these questions up during class or to your professor, which will give you a deeper understanding of the material. Especially in college, most professors have in-depth class discussions about the textbook readings. These discussions tend to count as a grade for class participation, so you want to make sure you are prepared and able to add your own opinion into the conversation.

Other Details While Studying a Textbook.
The information in a textbook will be easier to understand when you put it into your own words. This translation simplifies the text into terms that you are familiar with, so you can easily explain the information or answer questions. It improves your comprehension of the material and not just the memorization. Keeping

it in your own words is also helpful for when you need to write essays as it prevents the likelihood of plagiarizing.

Be creative when writing the questions and answers, so that you are engaged while studying. Create note cards or a study guide along with the text that you will understand and enjoy completing. Or come with up quizzes and games that you can exchange with a peer. Increase your learning pathways. Instead of just reading the text try visualizing, listening, or using a hands-on approach to learning. Simply reading and writing isn't an effective learning method for everyone.
Work with a partner. After you've done the reading and taken notes, try working with a peer to review the information. They could help you with difficult parts and quiz you to ensure comprehension. Also, if you are teaching or discussing the material with them, then you have a higher chance of being able to recall that information yourself.

> Read out loud. Hearing the words as you read with a physical voice—not just the one in your head—processes in your brain differently and increases your ability to remember.

> Use the keys in a textbook, the internet, or a dictionary to define any words or references that you do not know or struggle with to avoid confusion.

> If you are have trouble understanding the material, then seek help from your teacher, a tutor, or even a friend. Another fresh perspective can explain the concepts to you in a way you've never thought of before.

•

Conclusion

Congratulations! You have made it this far because you have applied yourself diligently to practicing for the exam and no doubt improved your potential score considerably! Passing your up-coming exam is a huge step in a journey that might be challenging at times but will be many times more rewarding and fulfilling. That is why being prepared is so important.

Good Luck!

REGISTER FOR FREE UPDATES AND MORE PRACTICE TEST QUESTIONS

Register your purchase at

https://www.test-preparation.ca/register/ for updates and free test tips and more practice test questions.

https://www.faceb............CompleteTestPreparation/

https://www.youtube.com/user/MrTestPreparation

ONLINE RESOURCES

How to Prepare for a Test - The Ultimate Guide

https://www.test-preparation.ca/prepare-test/

Learning Styles - The Complete Guide

https://www.test-preparation.ca/learning-style/

Test Anxiety Secrets!

https://www.test-preparation.ca/test-anxiety/

Time Management on a Test

https://www.test-preparation.ca/time-management/

Flash Cards - The Complete Guide

https://www.test-preparation.ca/flash-cards/

Test Preparation Video Series

https://www.test-preparation.ca/test-video/

How to Memorize - The Complete Guide

https://www.test-preparation.ca/memorize/

Online Library of Student Tips and Strategies

https://www.test-preparation.ca/students-say/

www.ingramcontent.com/pod-product-compliance
Lightning Source LLC
Chambersburg PA
CBHW061046110426
42740CB00049B/2468